20 Irresistible Reading-Response Projects Based on Favorite Picture Books

by Sherry Girard

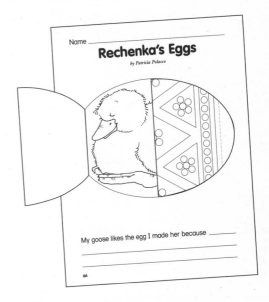

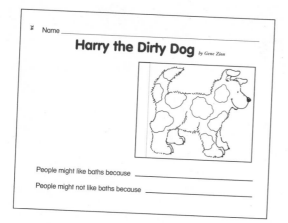

SCHOLASTIC
PROFESSIONAL BOOKS

New York • Toronto • London • Auckland • Sydney • Mexico City • New Delhi • Hong Kong • Buenos Aires

To my parents, Webb and Zelda, for reading to me, taking me to a library often, and continuing to share their love of finding a "good read."

Acknowledgments

To Dee Bowns, my good friend and mentor, for her generosity and encouragement throughout the development of this project. A special thanks to the wonderful Scholastic editors, Kama Einhorn and Deborah Schecter, for their assistance in smoothing out the rough edges and organizing this into a final manuscript.

Cover design by Norma Ortiz

Interior illustrations by Maxie Chambliss

Interior design by Ellen Matlach Hassell
for Boultinghouse & Boultinghouse, Inc.

ISBN: 0-439-20572-7

1 2 3 4 5 6 7 8 9 10   40   08 07 06 05 04 03 02 01

Contents

Introduction

Welcome to *20 Irresistible Reading-Response Projects Based on Favorite Picture Books*! This collection of 20 engaging projects is guaranteed to inspire young readers and writers.

It's easy to get started. First, you share a well-loved picture book with children. Then, they respond with a charming, do-it-yourself art project that they personalize with their own writing. You can then bind all children's pages into a collaborative class book, and presto! You have a keepsake of the many responses children have to their favorite stories.

After the class has completed a collaborative book, you can:

✳ Read each page as a group, so that children become familiar with the sentence frame on each page.

✳ Read with an individual child as an informal assessment.

✳ Put the books in the library corner for children to read and enjoy again and again.

✳ Donate them to your school library.

✳ Send them home for children to share with their families (put them into large self-sealing plastic bags).

✳ Organize a book fair and invite other classes to come read your creations!

✳ Unbind the books at the end of the year and create individual collections of children's work!

What's Inside

For each project, you'll find:

Before You Read: As you preview the book, pose these questions to help children build background and draw on their previous experience.

After You Read: After enjoying the book together as a group, refer to the discussion topics and guiding questions to help children process their story experience.

The Reading-Response Activity: Each activity gives you step-by-step instructions for a charming art and writing project. Children customize their project by completing a simple sentence frame with their own idea about the story.

Materials: This list includes all the easy-to-find materials you'll need to complete the activity.

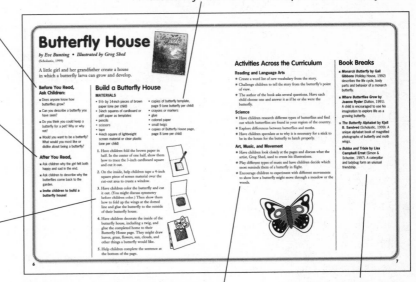

Activities Across the Curriculum: This section provides extension activities to enrich children's story experience.

Book Breaks: This feature offers books on related themes.

Ready-to-Use Reproducible Pages: Each project includes simple patterns for you to copy and give to each child. A reading-response page includes a sentence frame with a blank space for children to fill in—an easy-to-use framework for children's early writing experiences!

Ways to Bind the Books

* Punch holes and bind with metal rings.
* Punch holes and bind with yarn, ribbon, or string.
* Use brass fasteners for shorter books.
* Use plastic binders (you'll need a bookbinding machine).
* Bind pages into a hardcover three-ring binder.

Please Note: Four of the 20 project pages (*Yoko, Verdi, Poppleton,* and *Strega Nona*) will be three-dimensional, making them difficult to bind together into books; instead, you might display these completed pages on a bulletin board.

Butterfly House

by Eve Bunting • Illustrated by Greg Shed

(Scholastic, 1999)

A little girl and her grandfather create a house in which a butterfly larva can grow and develop.

Before You Read, Ask Children:

- Does anyone know how butterflies grow?

- Can you describe a butterfly you have seen?

- Do you think you could keep a butterfly for a pet? Why or why not?

- Would you want to be a butterfly? What would you most like or dislike about being a butterfly?

After You Read,

- Ask children why the girl felt both happy and sad in the end.

- Ask children to describe why the butterflies come back to the garden.

- **Invite children to build a butterfly house!**

Build a Butterfly House

MATERIALS

- 5½- by 14-inch pieces of brown paper (1 per child)
- 3-inch squares of cardboard or stiff paper as templates
- pencils
- scissors
- tape
- 4-inch square of lightweight screen material or clear plastic (1 per child)
- copies of butterfly template, page 9 (1 butterfly per child)
- crayons or markers
- glue
- colored paper
- small twigs
- copies of Butterfly House page, page 8 (1 per child)

1. Have children fold the brown paper in half. In the center of one half, show them how to trace the 3-inch cardboard square and cut it out.

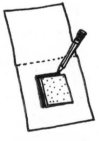

2. On the inside, help children tape a 4-inch square piece of screen material over the cutout area to create a window.

3. Have children color the butterfly and cut it out. (You might discuss symmetry before children color.) Then show them how to fold up the wings at the dotted lines and glue the butterfly to the outside of their butterfly house.

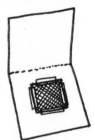

4. Have children decorate the inside of the butterfly house, including a twig, and glue the completed home to their Butterfly House page. They might draw leaves, grass, flowers, sun, clouds, and other things a butterfly would like.

5. Help children complete the sentence at the bottom of the page.

Activities Across the Curriculum

Reading and Language Arts

✳ Create a word list of new vocabulary from the story.

✳ Challenge children to tell the story from the butterfly's point of view.

✳ The author of the book asks several questions. Have each child choose one and answer it as if he or she were the butterfly.

Science

✳ Have children research different types of butterflies and find out which butterflies are found in your region of the country.

✳ Explore differences between butterflies and moths.

✳ Have children speculate why it is necessary for a stick to be in the house for the butterfly to hatch properly.

Art, Music, and Movement

✳ Have children look closely at the pages and discuss what the artist, Greg Shed, might have used to create his illustrations.

✳ Play different types of music and have children decide which most reminds them of a butterfly in flight.

✳ Encourage children to experiment with different movements to show how a butterfly might move through a meadow or the woods.

Book Breaks

■ *Monarch Butterfly* **by Gail Gibbons** (Holiday House, 1992) describes the life cycle, body parts, and behavior of a monarch butterfly.

■ *Where Butterflies Grow* **by Joanne Ryder** (Dutton, 1991). A child is encouraged to use his imagination to explore life as a growing butterfly.

■ *The Butterfly Alphabet* **by Kjell B. Sandved** (Scholastic, 1999). A unique alphabet book of magnified photographs of butterfly and moth wings.

■ *Bubba and Trixie* **by Lisa Campbell Ernst** (Simon & Schuster, 1997). A caterpillar and ladybug form an unusual friendship.

Butterfly House

by Eve Bunting

When my butterfly is set free, it will fly to _____

_____

_____

20 Irresistible Reading-Response Projects Based on Favorite Picture Books   Scholastic Professional Books

Butterfly House

Old Black Fly

by Jim Aylesworth • *Illustrated by Stephen Gammell*
(Henry Holt, 1992)

This rhyming alphabet book follows a mischievous fly all around the house.

Before You Read, Ask Children:

■ What do flies sound like?

■ Would you like to be a fly? Why or why not?

■ Would you like to have a fly for a pet? Why or why not?

After You Read,

■ List on chart paper the things the fly landed on during his adventure. How many can children remember?

■ Ask children: *If the fly could talk, what would he say about his adventure? What would he like best? What would he find scary or funny? What would he encounter while flying through your room at home?*

■ **Invite children to make their own "flyswatter"!**

Swat That Fly!

MATERIALS
• copies of page 12 (1 per child)
• crayons
• construction paper
• scissors
• glue stick
• plastic flies (or drawing supplies)
• pencils

1. Have children draw a line on their page in crayon, from letter to letter in alphabetical order.

2. Have children trace their hands onto construction paper, cut out their hand shape, and fold a flap at the wrist.

3. Glue the flap of the hand onto the sheet and have children add a plastic fly (or draw one) anywhere under the hand. Children then complete the sentence at the bottom of the page, filling in the blank with the letter on which they have glued or drawn their fly.

Activities Across the Curriculum

Reading and Language Arts

* On chart paper, brainstorm a list of adjectives that describe flies and write a collaborative poem using those words.

* Make a class insect alphabet book. Each child takes a sheet of paper with a letter of the alphabet, provides an insect-related word and illustration, and contributes one page of a whole-class book. You might share *A My Name Is Alice* by Jane Bayer or *The Icky Bug Book* by Jerry Polatta as inspiration for this project.

Math and Science

* Help children define *pest* and understand or find out why flies are considered pests.

* Read nonfiction books about flies and make a list titled "Fly Facts."

* Looking back at the story, ask children: How many members of the family did the fly visit? How many pets did this family own?

Art, Music, and Movement

* Have children speculate about how Stephen Gammell might have created his illustrations.

* Place several small blobs of tempera paint on a large sheet of white construction paper. Then place a piece of plastic wrap lightly over the blobs. Children can "smack" the blobs with their hands to create the splat effect used in the book. (Demonstrate this by making a fist and using the bottom part of the hand.)

* Play music and have children demonstrate the movement of a fly!

Book Links

■ *There Was an Old Lady Who Swallowed a Fly* by Simms Taback (Viking, 1997). This Caldecott Honor book is a new take on an old favorite.

■ *The Thing That Bothered Farmer Brown* by Teri Sloat (Orchard, 1995). In his attempt to get rid of a pesky mosquito, Farmer Brown succeeds in awakening all the animals!

■ *Gotcha!* by Gail Jorgenson (Scholastic, 1997). When Bertha Bear is ready to cut her birthday cake, a pesky fly does its best to disturb the celebration!

Name _____

Old Black Fly

by Jim Aylesworth

A C E F

B

K D I H

G

L J

W X

M N O

V Y

Q P T

R S U Z

This fly landed on or near the letter _____.

Verdi

by *Janell Cannon*

(Harcourt, 1997)

A young snake is supposed to change color as he grows to be big and strong—but doesn't really want to grow up!

Before You Read, Ask Children:

- Have you ever seen or touched a snake? What did it look or feel like?

- Would you like to have a snake for a pet? Why or why not?

- What does your family do for you to help you grow up big and strong?

- What is good or not so good about being little? What is good or not so good about being grown up?

After You Read,

- Ask, *Why do you think Verdi didn't want to turn green?*

- Ask, *If you could ask Verdi any question, what would it be?*

- **Invite children to re-create Verdi and his pals in a jungle scene!**

Verdi's Pals

MATERIALS

- 4- by 8-inch sheets of green and brown construction paper (1 of each per child)
- scissors
- copies of page 15 (1 per child)
- glue
- green and yellow pipe cleaners (2 yellow, 1 green per child)
- cylindrical objects about 1 inch in diameter (such as glue sticks, film canisters, and blocks)
- yellow and green paper scraps
- crayons
- "wiggly" eyes (available in craft stores)
- strong clear tape (such as packing tape)
- pencils

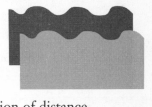

1. Help children cut the construction paper to resemble large hills and glue them to their page, placing the brown hill in the background to give the illusion of distance.

2. To curl the snakes, help children wrap the pipe cleaners around a cylindrical object.

3. To create the heads of the snakes, children trace around their thumbs on scraps of green and yellow paper, cut out the shape they traced, add eyes and other facial features, and tape them onto the pipe cleaners.

4. Children tape their snakes onto their page, first carefully tucking the tails underneath the hills.

5. Invite children to complete the sentence at the bottom of their page.

Activities Across the Curriculum

Reading and Language Arts

✳ Discuss Bumble and let children describe Verdi through Bumble's eyes. Have them explain what Bumble might have thought about Verdi's behavior.

✳ Help children copy, complete, and illustrate the sentence "When I grow up I want to be a _____." Bind all pages into a class book.

✳ Help children create a list of words on chart paper that could be used to describe a snake. Together, form alliterative phrases (*Sleek, slinky, slimy, slithery snakes!*).

Math and Science

✳ Together, read nonfiction books about snakes and make a list on chart paper titled "Snake Facts."

✳ Verdi and his friends did some things that snakes cannot really do. Ask children to name those activities and speculate about why snakes can't do these things. What animals might be able to jump from tree to tree?

✳ Find out about the snakes found in your area and give children adding-machine tape to create life-size models of those snakes.

✳ Have children attempt to remove a sock from their hands without assistance or the use of their other hand. Ask: *How long did it take? What skills did you need to remove the sock? What might this have to do with snakes?* Guide children to understand how and why snakes shed their skin.

Art, Music, and Movement

✳ After examining Janell Cannon's illustrations, let children speculate about how she creates the very soft tones.

✳ Play some of the composer Verdi's music and have children slither to the music like snakes!

✳ Give children each a 6-inch piece of string and have them imagine that it's a snake. They can dip the string in paint and pull it with wiggly, squiggly motions across a sheet of construction paper.

Book Links

■ *Hide and Snake* **by Keith Baker** (Harcourt, 1991). A snake is "hidden" in each bold jungle illustration!

■ *Crictor* **by Tomi Ungerer** (HarperCollins, 1984). A very intelligent boa constrictor goes to school, plays with the children, and protects his owner from a burglar.

Verdi

by Janell Cannon

Name _____

I would like to be able to _____

_____ like Verdi.

The Very Quiet Cricket

by Eric Carle

(Putnam, 1997)

A very quiet cricket wants to make a sound—and finally gets his wish!

Before You Read, Ask Children:

- Have you ever seen or heard a cricket? What do crickets look and sound like?

- How do you think crickets make their sounds?

- Do you think you could keep a cricket for a pet?

- Do you think insects "talk" to each other?

After You Read,

- Ask children how they think the cricket felt, not being able to make a sound.

- Ask, *What do you think the cricket wanted to say?*

- **Invite children to create their very own cricket music!**

Cricket Music

MATERIALS

- 1- by 6-inch long strips of sandpaper (2 per child)
- hole puncher
- scissors
- brass fastener
- copies of page 18 (1 per child)
- crayons
- pencils

1. Help children punch a hole in one end of each sandpaper strip, trim them to look like rounded wings, and then fasten them together with a brass fastener (the rough sides of the sandpaper face each other).

2. Have children color the cricket picture on their page and then use the brass fastener to attach the wings to the dot on the cricket.

3. Children can complete the sentence at the bottom of the page.

Activities Across the Curriculum

Reading and Language Arts

✳ Enjoy other Eric Carle classics, such as *The Tiny Seed*, *Pancakes, Pancakes!*, and *The Very Hungry Caterpillar*.

✳ Ask students to choose one of the animals from the story and pretend to be that animal, making the sound it made during its encounter with the cricket.

✳ To compare "loud" and "quiet," have children cut out pictures from old magazines that somehow illustrate each word and paste them to two different sheets of poster board, one labeled "Loud" and the other "Quiet." Using those illustrations, children can make up and share various similes: *Loud as a _____* or *Quiet as a _____*. You might post the "Quiet" poster in the quiet area.

Math and Science

✳ Ask children, *What other insects besides crickets make noise?*

✳ Help children create a list of the kinds of insects found where you live. Compare that list to insects found in the story.

✳ Visit Eric Carle's Web site: http://www.ericcarle.com

Art, Music, and Movement

✳ Have children explore Eric Carle's artistic style by making a collage of tissue paper. Cut different colors of tissue paper into various simple shapes. Children paint a piece of paper with a thin layer of liquid starch and lay the tissue paper shapes over it, overlapping as desired to create different effects.

✳ Encourage children to use sand blocks or other musical instruments to re-create the sounds from the story.

✳ Invite children to move around the room like crickets!

Book Links

■ *A Pocketful of Cricket* by **Rebecca Caudill** (Henry Holt, 1993). A young boy befriends a cricket.

■ *I Wish I Were a Butterfly* by **Jane Howe** (Harcourt, 1994). A young cricket wishes he were a butterfly, and a wise old spider helps him see that beauty is found within.

■ *Quick as a Cricket* by **Audrey Wood** (Child's Play International, 1990). A vibrant celebration of one child's self-discovery.

Name

The Very Quiet Cricket

by Eric Carle

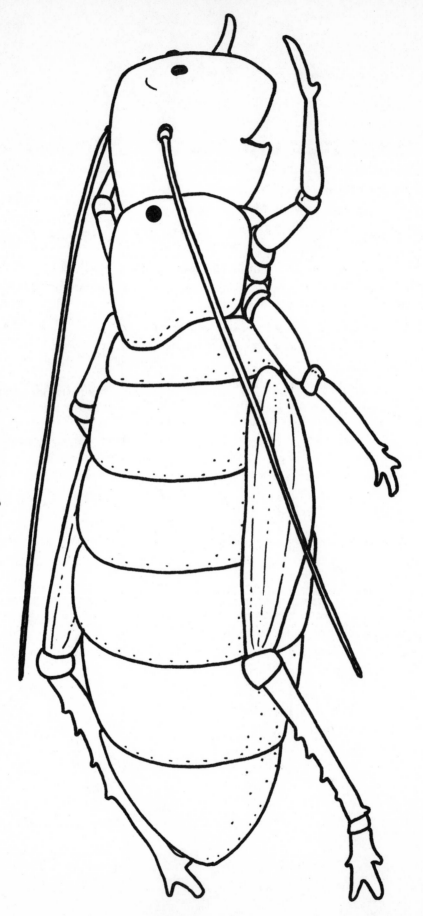

My cricket is trying to say

20 Irresistible Reading-Response Projects Based on Favorite Picture Books   Scholastic Professional Books

Strega Nona

by Tomie de Paola

(Aladdin, 1988)

Strega Nona has a magic pasta pot—
and Big Anthony wants some pasta!

Before You Read, Ask Children:

■ Have you ever seen this medal? (Point to the Caldecott medal.) Does anyone know what it means?

■ Can you find Italy on the globe or map?

■ What is pasta? Does anyone know how it is made?

■ What sort of pasta do you like to eat?

After You Read,

■ Ask children, *What advice would you give to Big Anthony next time he wants to try one of Strega Nona's magic tricks?*

■ Ask, *Would you like to have eaten all that pasta?*

■ Ask, *What do you think Strega Nona meant when she said "the punishment must fit the crime"?*

■ **Invite children to create their very own pot of pasta!**

Strega Nona's Pasta Pot

MATERIALS

• copies of page 21 (1 per child)
• crayons
• pencils
• dry pasta in various shapes and colors
• glue

1. Invite children to color the pasta pot and glue various kinds of pasta onto the pot.

2. Help children complete the sentence at the bottom of the page. You might first write the name of each type of pasta on chart paper for reference.

Name _____

Strega Nona
by Tomie DePaola

My favorite kind of pasta is _____

Activities Across the Curriculum

Reading and Language Arts

✳ On chart paper, write the directions for making your favorite food and share it with children. Don't forget to include the three kisses in your recipe! Then have a child explain to you how his or her favorite food is prepared and write out the recipe as he or she speaks.

✳ Have children retell the story from Big Anthony's or another villager's point of view.

✳ Ask children, *If you could do something magical, what would it be?* Make a list on chart paper of their responses.

✳ Make a list of the Italian words found in the story: *grazie*—thank you, *si*—yes, *strega*—witch, *nona*—grandma, *pasta*. Does anyone in the class speak Italian? Does anyone know how to say *thank you, grandma,* or *yes* in another language?

Math and Science

✳ Gather various kinds of pasta. Then have students compare the pasta according to size, shape, or color. Or sort by color or shape and graph the results.

✳ Leave a piece of dry pasta in a cup of water overnight. What happens? Why?

✳ Invite a parent in to make pasta with a pasta machine! Cook the pasta and share with the class.

Art, Music, and Movement

✳ Have children make noodle necklaces by stringing pasta onto a piece of yarn. You might first paint the noodles different colors, using nontoxic paint.

✳ Have children pretend to be long strands of pasta being cooked, prepared, and eaten!

Book Links

■ *Strega Nona: Her Story* by **Tomie de Paola** (Putnam, 1996). Strega Nona tells her own life story in a prequel to *Strega Nona*.

■ *Big Anthony: His Story* by **Tomie de Paola** (Putnam, 1998). Follow Big Anthony from his birth to the time he knocks on Strega Nona's door looking for a job.

■ *Strega Nona Meets Her Match* by **Tomie de Paola** (Putnam, 1993). When Strega Amelia comes to town, she begins to compete with Strega Nona by using new techniques and equipment. Things do not look good for Strega Nona—until Strega Amelia hires Big Anthony.

Name _____

Strega Nona
by Tomie de Paola

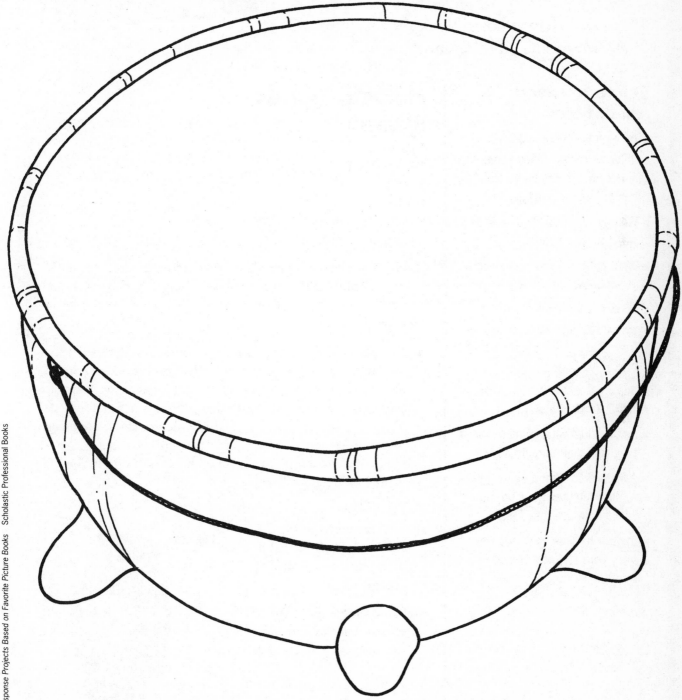

My favorite kind of pasta is _____

Hands

by Lois Ehlert

(Harcourt, 1997)

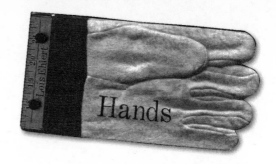

This hand-shaped board book shows hands of all sizes doing all different things.

Before You Read, Ask Children:

- Do people's ages make a difference in how their hands look or the things their hands can do? Why or why not?

- What kinds of things do people wear on their hands?

- What activities can you do with your hands?

- Look at your hands. How are your hands the same or different from those of the person sitting next to you?

After You Read,

- Ask children what kinds of things they help their parents do.

- Ask children what they would like to do when they grow up. How would it involve their hands?

- **Invite children to make their very own *Helping Hands* book!**

Helping Hands

MATERIALS

- pencils
- colored paper
- scissors
- hole puncher
- copies of page 24 (1 per child)
- brass fasteners (2 per child)

1. Have children use pencils and colored paper to trace a hand of each of their family members at home (the fingers should be close together, not spread apart), cut out each, and bring them to school.

2. In class, help children arrange the hands in order of size, with the biggest at the bottom of the pile. Discuss what each person whose hand was traced does with his or her hands to help at home. On each hand, children complete the sentence "My _____ is good at _____." (For younger children you can write this sentence frame several times on one sheet of paper, then copy and cut it apart so that children can fill in the blanks and glue to their page.)

3. Punch holes in the wrist of each hand and help children attach the hands to their page with a brass fastener.

4. Children complete the sentence at the bottom of the page.

Activities Across the Curriculum

Reading and Language Arts

* Have children cut out pictures of hands from magazines or newspapers and create a collage of hands. Discuss the activities that are represented (cooking, hammering, caring for a child, and so on) and label each picture with a self-sticking note.

* Brainstorm a list of everyday jobs and tasks that can be done only by using hands.

* Hands can be used to deliver messages without words! Ask children to list and demonstrate some common hand signals (come here, stop, this way, be quiet).

* Share some words or letters in sign language.

Math and Science

* Explore the sense of touch. Gather objects of different textures (such as cotton, sandpaper, a marble, and aluminum foil) and place them in a paper bag. Then have children feel the objects, describe what they feel like, and try to name them.

* Children can use their hands as a nonstandard measurement to measure the length of the classroom, the height of their desks, each other, the size of their chairs and books, and so on.

* Since there are two hands per person in the classroom, children can sit in a circle, hold up their hands, and practice counting by 2s.

Art, Music, and Movement

* Give each child a lump of clay to roll and flatten. They can press their hands into the clay surface to leave an imprint. Have them write their name in the clay with a pencil.

* Have children press their palms or fingertips onto an inkpad and create a design or picture with the print they leave on the paper. Examine fingerprints.

* Create patterns by clapping and imitating repeated rhythms as a whole group, small group, or paired activity. Children can take turns leading.

Book Links

* ***My Hands* by Aliki** (HarperCollins, 1999). A delightful book that explores all the different ways we use our hands each day.

* ***Piggies* by Audrey Wood** (Harcourt, 1991). Follow the antics of ten piggies getting ready for bed.

Name _____

Hands

by Lois Ehlert

When I grow up, I would like to be a _____

I would use my hands for _____

_____

20 Irresistible Reading-Response Projects Based on Favorite Picture Books   Scholastic Professional Books

The Patchwork Quilt

by Valerie Flournoy • *Illustrated by Jerry Pinkney*

(Pearson Learning, 1985)

A young girl creates a special family quilt with her mother and grandmother.

Before You Read, Ask Children:

- Does your family have a special quilt, or do you have a quilt or blanket of your own?

- How do you think a quilt is put together? How long do you think it would take to make a quilt? What do you think quilts are made of?

- What else could you make with a grandparent?

After You Read,

- Ask children, *How do you think Tanya's grandmother felt, not being able to work on the quilt?*

- Ask, *If you were Tanya, what would you have said when Mother and Grandmother gave you the quilt?*

- **Invite children to participate in a quilting bee, and have them design their very own quilt square!**

Quilting Bee

MATERIALS

- copies of page 27 (1 per child)
- different colors of construction paper (cut into 2-inch squares and some 2-inch squares cut in half diagonally into triangles)
- glue sticks

1. Help children explore different ways to make a pattern within the quilt outline. Demonstrate different combinations of colors and shapes.

2. After children have practiced forming several different patterns, they can glue down their pieces in a design of their choice.

3. Children complete the sentence at the bottom of the page.

 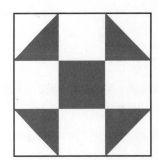

 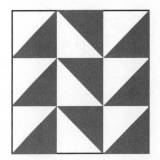

Activities Across the Curriculum

Reading and Language Arts

✳ Explore the letter *Qq*! List other words that begin with *Qq* and point out that it is always followed by a *u*.

✳ Have each child complete a "listening quilt." Pass out large squares of white paper and instruct children to fold them in half four times to create 16 small squares within the big square. Give the following directions verbally, one at a time. Then display the quilts on a bulletin board.

> Put red hearts in each corner square.
> Write your name in one square.
> Draw blue stripes in two squares.
> Draw red dots in three squares.
> Draw green dots in three squares.
> In one square, draw two yellow flowers.
> In one square, draw anything you like.

Math and Science

✳ Take a survey to find out how many children have a handmade quilt at home. Invite them to bring the quilts to school to share.

✳ If everyone in the class contributed one block to a perfectly square quilt, how many rows across or down would the quilt be? Would anyone have to make an extra square in order to complete a row?

Art, Music, and Movement

✳ Instead of binding children's pages into a book, trim around the edges of each square and create a whole-class quilt made from squares designed by each student.

✳ Design a class quilt that represents your school or community.

Book Links

■ *Quilt-Block History of Pioneer Days With Projects Kids Can Make* by Mary Cobb (Millbrook, 1995) is full of step-by-step quilt patterns and easy-to-make quilt projects for children.

■ *The Keeping Quilt* by Patricia Polacco (Simon & Schuster, 1998). This charming story traces a family's history through a dress that is eventually made into a family quilt.

■ *Sam Johnson and the Blue-Ribbon Quilt* by Lisa Campbell Ernst (William Morrow, 1983). Sam Johnson likes quilting so much, he wants to join his wife's quilting circle! When his wife refuses, Sam gathers the men to form their own club.

■ *Sweet Clara and the Freedom Quilt* by Deborah Hopkinson (Knopf, 1993). By saving scraps of materials and listening, a slave stitches a quilt that becomes a map to freedom.

■ *Luka's Quilt* by Gloria Guback (Greenwillow, 1994). Luka's grandmother creates a quilt in the traditional Hawaiian custom of using one color—but Luka wants a colorful quilt!

Name _____

The Patchwork Quilt
by Valerie Flournoy

I would like my own quilt because _____

_____

20 Irresistible Reading-Response Projects Based on Favorite Picture Books   Scholastic Professional Books

Koala Lou

by Mem Fox • Illustrated by Pamela Lofts

(Harcourt, 1994)

Koala Lou competes in the Bush Olympics, in hopes that her mother will remind her how much she loves her!

Before You Read, Ask Children:

- How do you show someone you love him or her?

- Can you think of a time you worked really hard at something?

- Where is Australia? Find it on a map or globe.

- Do you know what the Olympics are?

After You Read,

- Ask children what they thought about the ending of the story.

- Ask, *If you were Koala Lou, what might you have done differently?*

- **Invite children to create their very own hug for Koala Lou!**

A Hug for Koala Lou

MATERIALS

- copies of pages 30–31 (1 of each per child)
- crayons
- scissors
- glue sticks
- scrap materials
- pencils

1. Ask children to color and cut out the koalas and arms, then fold the arms forward on the lines.

2. Have children draw (or create from scrap materials and glue) a tree for Koala Lou and her mother to sit in.

3. Help children glue the arms onto their pages colored side down so they're open and the thumbs are facing up. They then glue Koala Lou and her mother on top of the arms. Then have children fold the arms around Lou for a big koala hug.

4. Children complete the sentence at the bottom of their page.

Activities Across the Curriculum

Reading and Language Arts

✳ What other words rhyme with *Lou, do,* and *you*? Make a list and write a collaborative poem to Koala Lou.

✳ Find words in the book specific to Australia and create an "Australian Words" list on chart paper.

✳ As a group, write an acrostic poem using the word *koala*.

✳ Write a letter to someone special telling how much you love him or her.

✳ Discuss ways of showing love to someone without saying it.

Math and Science

✳ What other animals are found in this book? What is a marsupial?

✳ What other animals live only in Australia? What animals live in your area that are not found anywhere else?

✳ Share nonfiction books and, as a class, list facts about koalas. Help children determine the closest place they might see koalas.

✳ Visit Mem Fox at her Web site: http://www.memfox.net

Art, Music, and Movement

✳ Like hugs, hearts are also used as a symbol of love. Let children construct heart mobiles using paper, pipe cleaners, wire, aluminum foil, and so on. Provide lace, bows, ribbon, and glitter for added pizzazz.

✳ Find out which sports are featured in the real Olympics. Which event would be most similar to "Bush Tree Climbing"?

✳ Invite children to move around the room like koalas!

Book Links

■ *Mama, Do You Love Me?* **by Barbara Joose** (Chronicle Books, 1991). A delightful story about a little girl who asks again and again if her mother loves her.

■ *I Love You the Purplest* **by Barbara Joose** (Chronicle Books, 1996). When two boys ask their mother to tell whom she loves the best, she comes up with a colorful, loving answer.

■ *Guess How Much I Love You* **by Sam McBratney** (Candlewick Press, 1995). Little Nutbrown Hare and his dad share a special day.

Name _____

Koala Lou

by Mem Fox

A hug from _____

makes me feel _____

20 Irresistible Reading-Response Projects Based on Favorite Picture Books   Scholastic Professional Books

Koala Lou

Lilly's Purple Plastic Purse

by Kevin Henkes

(Greenwillow, 1996)

Lilly can hardly wait to share her new purse and its contents with her class.

Before You Read, Ask Children:

- Can you think of a time when you could hardly wait to share something?

- What do you like about school?

- Do you have a special bag you carry things in?

- Can you think of something you once did that you were sorry for later?

After You Read,

- Ask, *What would you have done if you were Lilly and you couldn't wait to share your special thing?*

- Ask, *If you were Lilly, what would you keep in your purse?*

- **Invite children to make Lilly's purse!**

Let's Make Lilly's Purse

MATERIALS

- copies of pages 34–35 (1 of each per child)
- crayons (including plenty of purple ones!)
- scissors
- pencils
- glue sticks
- stickers or stamps

1. Have children decorate, color, and cut out the purse flap.

2. On the inside of the purse, children draw items that Lilly may have carried to school.

3. Help children glue the top edge of the purse to the paper so that the purse "opens."

4. Children complete the sentence at the bottom of the page.

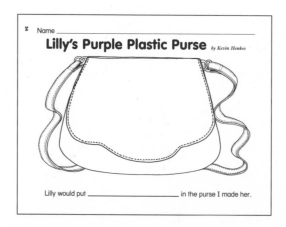

Activities Across the Curriculum

Reading and Language Arts

✳ Have children retell the story from the perspective of another child in Lilly's class.

✳ Write a collaborative apology note to Mr. Slinger from Lilly.

✳ Have children list the things they would like to bring in to share. Write their ideas on chart paper.

✳ Together, find and list all the adjectives in the story on chart paper.

Math and Science

✳ Fill a purse with small items and have children estimate how many items are in the purse. As a group, count the items by 1s, 2s, 5s, or 10s to determine the exact number.

✳ Together, make "tasty cheese snacks," such as grilled cheese sandwiches.

Art, Music, and Movement

✳ Using scraps of paper, fabric, crayons, markers, and so on, children can design an outrageous hat or purse for Lilly or a new shirt for Mr. Slinger.

✳ Have children imitate Lilly's performance as she shares her purse with the group.

Book Links

■ *The Lady With the Alligator Purse* by Nadine Bernard Westcott (Little, Brown, 1990). A new version of an old jump rope favorite.

■ *The Purse* by Kathy Caple (Sandpiper, 1992). Katie spends her money on a new purse—but now has no money to put inside!

Lilly's Purple Plastic Purse

by Kevin Henkes

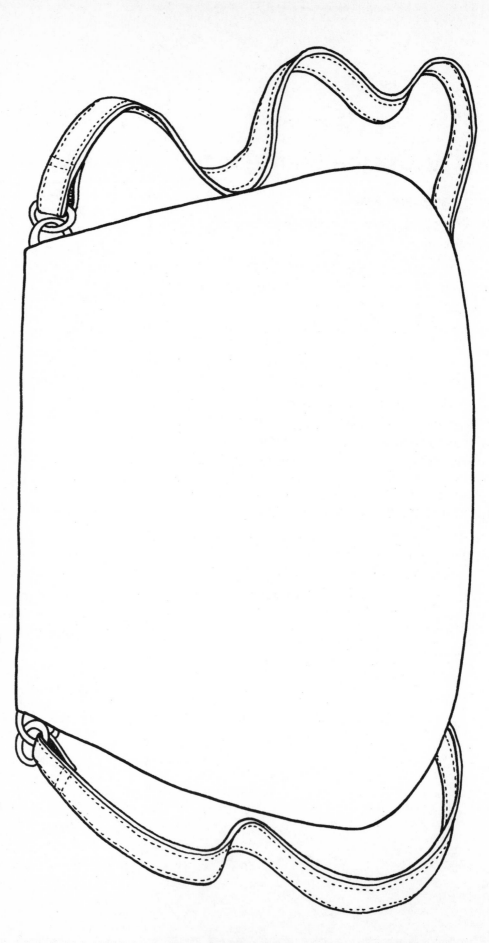

Lilly would put _____

_____ in the purse I made her.

20 Irresistible Reading-Response Projects Based on Favorite Picture Books Scholastic Professional Books

Lilly's Purple Plastic Purse

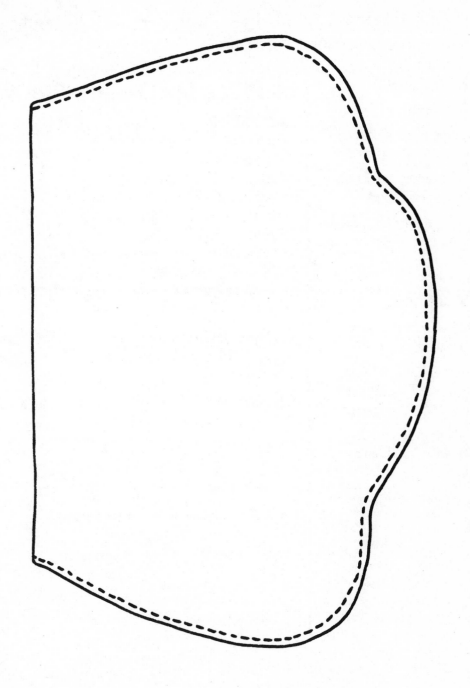

Owen

by Kevin Henkes

(Greenwillow, 1993)

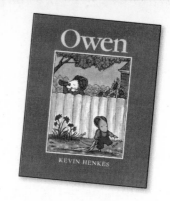

Owen wants to keep his prized blanket with him as he starts school for the first time.

Before You Read, Ask Children:

- Do you have a favorite blanket or stuffed animal? What is its name?

- Is there something special you like to carry in your pocket?

- When you started school, did you want to bring something special with you?

After You Read,

- Ask children what they think about the ending.

- Ask children what they would have done about the blanket if they were Owen or his parents.

- **Invite children to create a special place for Owen's blanket!**

A Place for Owen's Blanket

MATERIALS
- copies of page 38 (1 per child)
- crayons
- glue
- black beads or beans (2 per child)
- small pink pompoms (1 per child)
- yarn
- regular letter-sized envelopes, sealed and cut in half (½ envelope per child)
- 3-inch squares of yellow felt (1 per child)
- pencils

1. Have children color Owen and then glue black beads or beans on his eyes, a pink pompom on his nose, and cut yarn on his whiskers.

2. Have children decorate the half envelope and glue it to the front of Owen's overalls open side facing up, as a "pocket."

3. Help children put their "blankets" (yellow felt) in the pocket.

4. Invite children to complete the sentence at the bottom of the page.

Name _____

Owen
by Kevin Henkes

Owen likes his handkerchief because _____

38

Activities Across the Curriculum

Reading and Language Arts

* Ask children, *Why was Owen's blanket named Fuzzy? What name would you give his blanket?* Make a list on chart paper of their responses.

* Gather favorite books, poems, and songs on the topic of mice to share with the class.

* Have children describe their favorite stuffed animal or blanket. List all the adjectives on chart paper.

* Some parts of growing up are not easy. Have each child complete the sentence frame: "When I was very young I couldn't _____, but now I can _____."

* Ask children each to bring in a photo showing themselves with a special blanket or toy. Display photos on a bulletin board and have children guess who's who!

Math and Science

* With an inkpad and fine-point markers, make thumbprint mice. Children can create patterns and sets of thumbprint mice on index cards and use these cards to count in multiples of 2, 5, and 10.

* Ask children, *If Owen's blanket was two feet by two feet and Mother cut his blanket into four- by four-inch squares, how many handkerchiefs did Owen have?* Help children use a ruler or yardstick to figure out the answer (36 squares).

Art, Music, and Movement

* Create a mouse bookmark, using felt for the body and ears and yarn for the tail.

* Design a new blanket for Owen.

Book Links

- ***Benjamin Bigfoot* by Mary Serfozo** (Margaret McElderry, 1993). Benjamin goes everywhere in his father's shoes—but now he's going to school for the first time!

- ***Geraldine's Blanket* by Holly Keller** (Morrow, 1988). When Geraldine's parents try to put away her baby blanket, she finds a variety of ways to keep it.

- ***Franklin's Blanket* by Paulette Bourgeois** (Kids Can Press, 1997). Franklin loses his blanket—and cannot sleep without it!

Name _____

Owen

by Kevin Henkes

Owen likes his handkerchief because _____

_____

20 Irresistible Reading-Response Projects Based on Favorite Picture Books Scholastic Professional Books

Frog and Toad Are Friends

by Arnold Lobel

(HarperCollins, 1970)

Frog and Toad share a wonderful friendship!

Before You Read, Ask Children:

- Just by looking at the cover of this book, can you decide which character is Toad and which one is Frog?

- What do you know about frogs and toads?

- What is hibernation?

After You Read,

- Ask children, *What do you think makes Frog and Toad such good friends?*

- **Invite children to create their very own version of Frog and Toad!**

Making Friends With Frog and Toad

MATERIALS

- copies of page 41 (1 per child)
- glue
- green and brown paper cut into 4-inch circles (1 of each per child)
- green and brown paper cut into 1-inch circles (2 of each per child)
- small yellow dot stickers (4 per child)
- black beads or dried beans (8 per child)
- scissors
- yarn
- pencils

1. Have children glue the large circles (Frog and Toad's heads) to their page, then add the smaller circles for eyes. Children then add the yellow dots to the eyes.

2. To complete the eyes, have children glue beans or beads to the eyes. The nose holes can be made the same way.

3. Children can glue pieces of yarn to create mouths.

4. Have children complete the sentence at the bottom of the page.

Activities Across the Curriculum

Reading and Language Arts

* When Frog was sick, he wanted Toad to tell him a story. Have each child think of a story that Toad might have liked to hear. Ask volunteers to share their stories with the class.

* Arnold Lobel received a Caldecott Honor Book Award and a Newbery Honor Book Award. Discuss each of these awards and ask children why they think Lobel received awards for this particular book.

* Challenge children to find words that begin with the letter *Ff* and or *Tt* in magazines or newspapers. They can cut out the words and glue them in the appropriate column on a class chart.

Math and Science

* Have children collect buttons from family, friends, and neighbors. Using the donated buttons, have children sort by color, size, shape, number of holes, and the type of materials used (wood, glass, plastic). Graph the results.

* Have children estimate how far they can jump. Let children jump and see how close they came to their estimates.

* Ask children to name some of the things that Toad tried to grow in his garden and then tell what they'd like to grow in their own garden.

* Create a Venn diagram to show the similarities and differences between frogs and toads.

Art, Music, and Movement

* Show children how to make a frog paperweight. Paint a round stone green, add wiggle eyes, and glue the rock frog to a green felt lily pad.

* Tell children that frogs leap and toads hop. Invite children to move around the room like frogs or toads!

Book Links

- ***Frog and Toad Together* by Arnold Lobel** (HarperCollins, 1972). In this tale, Frog and Toad battle a dragon, make cookies, and plant a garden.

- ***Frog and Toad All Year* by Arnold Lobel** (HarperCollins, 1976). This is truly a year-long celebration with these two friends!

- ***Days With Frog and Toad* by Arnold Lobel** (HarperCollins, 1984). Frog and Toad tell ghost stories, fly kites, and clean house.

Name _____

Frog and Toad Are Friends

by Arnold Lobel

Frog and Toad are friends because _____

_____

George and Martha

by James Marshall

(Houghton Mifflin, 1972)

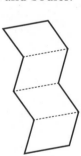

Two delightful hippo friends share adventures.

Before You Read, Ask Children:

■ What is a friend?

■ What do friends do for one another?

■ What sorts of things do you like to do with your friends?

■ Have you ever seen a hippopotamus?

After You Read,

■ Ask children how they think George and Martha got to be such good friends.

■ Have children speculate what George and Martha might do in the next chapter.

■ **Invite children to create their own happy hippos!**

Happy Hippo Friends

MATERIALS

• copies of pages 44–45 (1 of each per child)
• crayons
• scissors
• glue sticks
• wiggle eyes (available in craft stores)
• pencils

1. Have children color George's and Martha's heads and bodies.

2. Help children cut out George's and Martha's heads and the "accordion" strips. Show them how to fold the strips accordion style, glue one end onto the squares on the bodies and the other onto the back of the hippos' heads so that the heads "pop out" a bit.

3. Have children glue wiggle eyes onto George and Martha.

4. Invite children to complete the sentence at the bottom of the page.

George and Martha
by James Marshall

I like to _____ with my friends.

Activities Across the Curriculum

Reading and Language Arts

* Point out that this book has chapters. Can children think of any other chapter books?

* Gather some of James Marshall's other books so that children can explore his style of writing and illustration.

* Brainstorm a list of other things that George and Martha might enjoy doing together.

* Challenge children to use the letters in *hippopotamus* to build other words!

Math and Science

* Share nonfiction books and make a list of interesting hippo facts.

* Ask children to solve this problem: If George eats _____ pounds of plants a day and Martha eats _____ pounds of plants, how much do they eat in one day?

* Learn about herbivores or omnivores. Guide children to understand the difference between the two and, together, decide which describes George and Martha.

Art, Music, and Movement

* Have children create large portraits of George and Martha.

* Invite children to imitate hippos walking, dancing, or swimming!

* Sing songs about friendship.

Book Links

■ *George and Martha Encore* by **James Marshall** (Houghton Mifflin, 1973). George and Martha go to the beach, attend a dance recital, and wear disguises.

■ *George and Martha One Fine Day* by **James Marshall** (Houghton Mifflin, 1982). Five new stories about the adventures of the two friends.

Name _____

George and Martha

by James Marshall

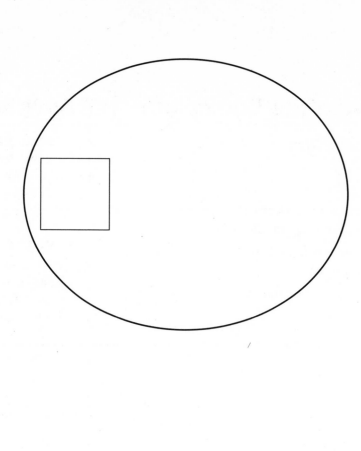

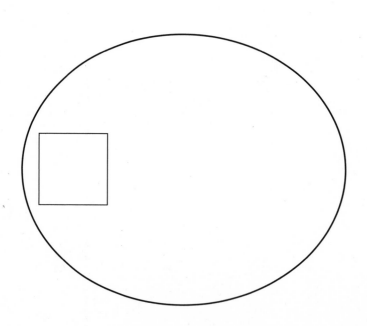

I like to _____ with my friends.

20 Irresistible Reading-Response Projects Based on Favorite Picture Books   Scholastic Professional Books

George and Martha

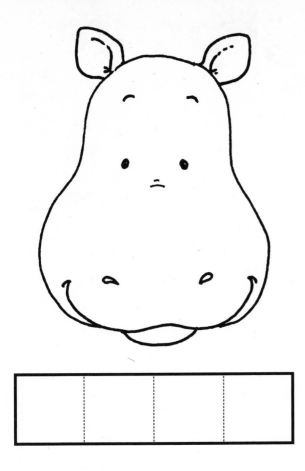

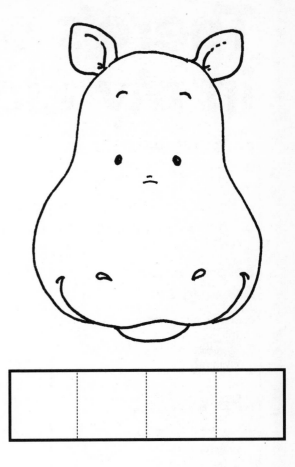

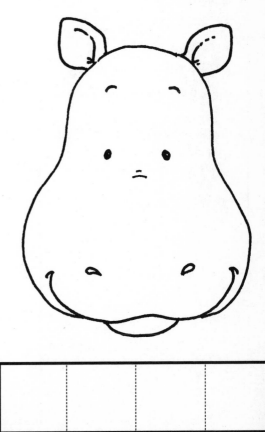

There's a Nightmare in My Closet

by Mercer Mayer

(Dutton, 1992)

A boy meets a large, scary monster living in his closet—but soon finds out that the monster is just as scared as he is!

Before You Read, Ask Children:

■ What is a nightmare?

■ What things have you been afraid of?

After You Read,

■ Ask, *How do you think the monster felt when he was hiding in the closet?*

■ Ask, *What would you have done if you were the boy?*

■ Ask, *Why do you think the boy and the monster became friends?*

■ **Invite children to create their very own monster!**

Monster-in-a-Closet Flip Book

MATERIALS
- copies of page 48 (1 per child)
- copies of page 49 (1 per child)
- crayons
- scissors
- glue sticks
- pencils
- 4½- by 6-inch pieces of construction paper (1 per child)

1. Have children color and decorate each of the three monsters differently and then cut along the outer solid black lines of the two monsters on page 49. Then they cut along the dotted lines, being careful not to cut all the way through the border.

2. Children glue their monsters, one at a time, onto their monster on page 48 (along the edge indicated).

3. Help children glue the construction paper "door." Glue along the edge so that it opens. When dry, children can flip back and forth to create their own mix-and-match monsters!

4. Invite children to name their monster and write its name at the bottom of the page.

Activities Across the Curriculum

Reading and Language Arts

✴ Write a collaborative letter to the monster explaining why it should or should not disappear.

✴ Have two children act out a conversation between two monsters that are afraid of a fly!

Math and Science

✴ With a variety of tangrams, let children create a "shape monster."

✴ Some monsters have big feet! Measure the length of each child's foot. Have children compare those figures and record them on a graph. Have children with different foot sizes "walk off" a given area and compare results.

✴ Brainstorm a list of animals that resemble a monster and have children explain why they think each animal is monsterlike.

✴ Make One-Eyed Monsters! Cut a hole from the center of a piece of bread. Butter the remaining bread and put it into a frying pan to brown. Break an egg into the hole, cook, and flip to cook the other side.

Art, Music, and Movement

✴ Listen to the song "Monster Mash" and encourage children to come up with some fun dance steps.

✴ Let children work in small groups to create a body part (specifically a head, upper body, and lower body) for a monster. Put the monsters together on a class bulletin board (there will be as many monsters as there are groups).

✴ Invite children to make monsters out of clay.

Book Links

■ *There's a Monster Under My Bed* by James Howe (Aladdin, 1990). Simon is convinced there is a monster under his bed!

■ *The Very Worst Monster* by Pat Hutchins (Morrow, 1985). No longer the center of attention after her baby brother is born, Hazel sets out to prove that she is the "Worst Monster in the World."

■ *There's an Alligator Under My Bed* by Mercer Mayer (Dutton, 1987). After discovering an alligator under his bed, a young boy devises a plan to lure the alligator into the garage.

Name _____

There's a Nightmare in My Closet

by Mercer Mayer

GLUE HERE

My monster's name: _____

20 Irresistible Reading-Response Projects Based on Favorite Picture Books   Scholastic Professional Books

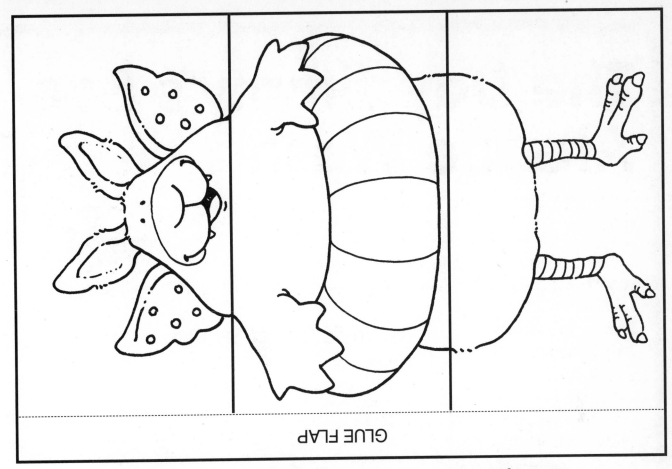

GLUE FLAP

There's a Nightmare in My Closet

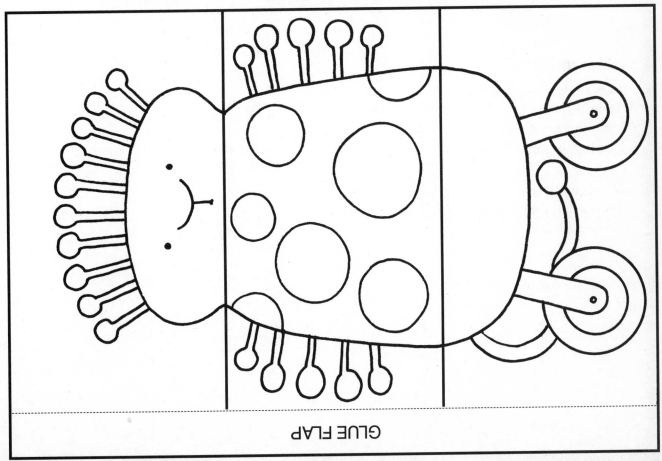

GLUE FLAP

The Day Jimmy's Boa Ate the Wash

by Trinka Hakes Noble • *Illustrated by Steven Kellogg*

(Pearson, 1992)

When a boy takes his pet snake on a school field trip to a farm, a series of mishaps occur!

Before You Read, Ask Children:

- What do you know about boa constrictors?

- Would you want a boa constrictor as a pet?

- Have you ever been on a farm? Does anyone here live on a farm?

- Do you think this story will be true or make-believe?

After You Read,

- Ask children to tell the story from the viewpoint of the boa, the farmer or his wife, the teacher, or the other farm animals.

- **Invite children to create their own colorful version of Jimmy's boa!**

Jimmy's Spiral Snake

MATERIALS
- copies of pages 52–53 (1 of each per child)
- crayons
- scissors
- glue sticks
- pencils

1. Have children color the snake and cut it out along the solid lines in a spiral.

2. Children glue the tip of the snake's tail to the main page so that the whole snake can be lifted up.

3. Invite children to complete the sentence at the bottom of their page.

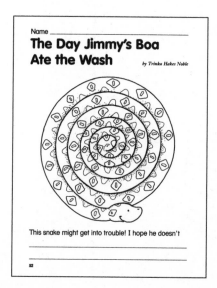

Activities Across the Curriculum

Reading and Language Arts

✳ Brainstorm a list of words associated with snakes (*slither, glide, silent, coiled, slimy*).

✳ If you could have Jimmy's boa take a trip, where would you want him to go? Write a new adventure for the snake.

✳ Make a list on chart paper of the chain of events (the cow cried because the haystack fell over, the haystack fell over because the farmer crashed into it, and so on).

Math and Science

✳ As a class, read some nonfiction books on snakes and list snake facts on chart paper.

✳ Estimate the length and weight of Jimmy's boa.

✳ Let children manipulate "slinky" metal coils and experiment with movement and measurement. Children might create a set of stairs or series of platforms for the slinkies to descend. Have children observe and discuss the differences between the sizes and materials of the slinkies as they move down the steps.

Art, Music, and Movement

✳ Make snakes by rolling clay into long logs.

✳ Invite children to slither, slide, and hiss like snakes!

Book Links

- ***Snake Alley Band* by Elizabeth Nygaard** (Bantam Doubleday, 1999). A snake gathers his friends to play in a hip-hoppin', splish-splashin', stamp-stompin' band!

- ***Hide and Snake* by Keith Baker** (Harcourt, 1995). A colorful snake hides in the illustrations as he slithers from page to page.

- ***Jimmy's Boa Bounces Back* by Trinka Hakes Noble** (Dutton, 1992). A disaster occurs when Jimmy's boa shows up at a fancy garden party!

- ***Jimmy's Boa and the Big Slash Birthday Bash* by Trinka Hakes Noble** (Dutton, 1989). Taking his boa to Sealand for a birthday celebration proves to be a rip-roaring adventure for Jimmy!

Name _____

The Day Jimmy's Boa Ate the Wash

by Trinka Hakes Noble

This snake might get into trouble! I hope he doesn't

_____

_____

20 Irresistible Reading-Response Projects Based on Favorite Picture Books   Scholastic Professional Books

The Day Jimmy's Boa Ate the Wash

If You Give a Moose a Muffin

by Laura Joffe Numeroff • *Illustrated by Felicia Bond*

(Pearson, 1991)

A silly, speculative tale of the crazy things that could happen if a moose were to get a muffin!

Before You Read, Ask Children:

- What do you think would happen if you gave a moose a muffin?
- What do moose eat?
- Where would you find a moose?
- Do you like muffins? What sort of muffins do you like?

After You Read:

- Discuss with the children what it means to have good manners. Help them list some words that a well-mannered character would use.
- Ask, *Now that you know what could happen if you gave a moose a muffin, would you give a moose a muffin? Why or why not?*
- **Invite children to make a moose and give him a muffin!**

Muffin for a Moose

MATERIALS
- copies of page 56 (1 per child)
- copies of page 57 (1 for every 6 children)
- crayons
- scissors
- glue sticks
- paper muffin cups (1 per child)
- watercolor paint or markers
- cotton balls
- pencils

1. Have children color the moose and then color and cut out the antlers.

2. Have children glue the antlers to the center of the moose's head, then bend the antlers forward so that they tilt away from the paper.

3. Have children glue the flat bottom of the muffin cup to their page so that it looks as if the moose is holding it.

4. Using watercolor paint or markers, children "dye" several cotton balls to be placed into the muffin cup (if using watercolors, let the cotton balls dry overnight). Children then glue the "muffins" into the cups.

5. Invite children to complete the sentence at the bottom of the page.

Activities Across the Curriculum

Reading and Language Arts

* Write out the lyrics to "The Muffin Man" on sentence strips and place them in a pocket chart.

* Together, write a story based on the pattern of this book, substituting an animal found in your area.

* Recording ideas on chart paper, help children create a dinner menu for a moose!

Math and Science

* Share nonfiction books about moose. What is their habitat? What do they feed on? Hhow big do they grow? What is the purpose of their antlers? Compare the similarities and differences with elk, deer, and caribou. On chart paper, make a list entitled "Moose Facts."

* Make muffins! First, make a list of different kinds of muffins and then vote on which one will be prepared. You might also create a favorite muffin recipe book.

* Challenge the class with "muffin math" (*2 muffins on the plate plus 3 more equals_____? There are 12 muffins on the plate and I took away 4. How many are left?*)

Art, Music, and Movement

* Help children make a moose puppet out of an old sock or a brown paper bag. Have them use their puppets to retell the story.

* Invite children to move around like moose!

* To create "moose prints," halve an apple and core it from top to bottom. Have children dip the cut side of the apple into paint, place it on the paper, and apply slight pressure. Lift it straight up to see the resulting hoof image. Have different-sized apples and various paints available to create a varied effect!

Book Links

* ***Moostache* by Margie Palatini** (Hyperion, 1997) is a fun-filled book about a moose with a gigantic moustache!

* ***Thidwick, the Big-Hearted Moose* by Dr. Seuss** (Random House, 1987). Kind, generous Thidwick finds that his enormous antlers are home to many animals!

* ***If You Give a Mouse a Cookie* by Laura Joffe Numeroff** (HarperCollins, 1985). A mouse wears a boy out with all his demands!

* ***If You Give a Pig a Pancake* by Laura Joffe Numeroff** (HarperCollins, 1998). A familiar but delightful adventure of dealing with a demanding, bossy pig.

If You Give a Moose a Muffin
by Laura Joffe Numeroff

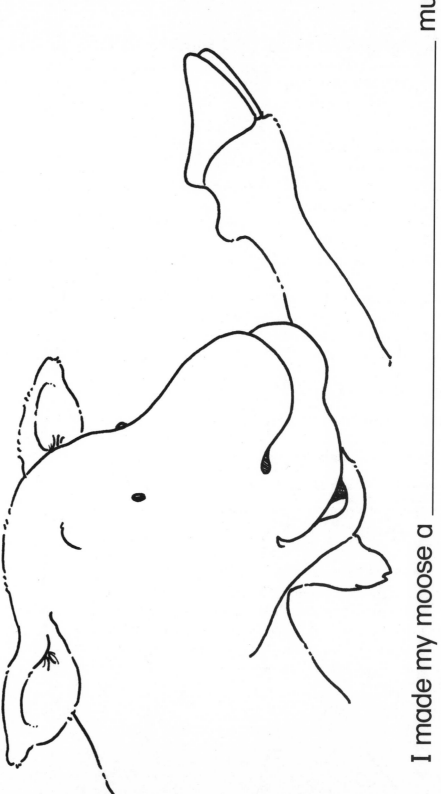

I made my moose a _____ muffin.

20 Irresistible Reading-Response Projects Based on Favorite Picture Books   Scholastic Professional Books

If You Give a Moose a Muffin

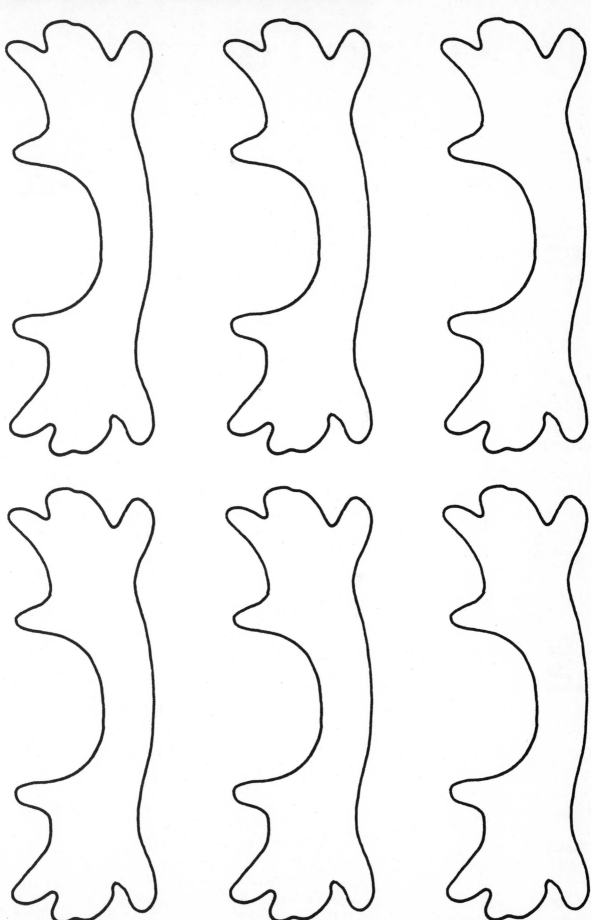

Just Plain Fancy

by Patricia Polacco

(Dell, 1994)

Naomi and Ruth, who live in an Amish community, discover a very fancy egg!

Before You Read, Ask Children:

- Can anyone find Pennsylvania on a map?

- Has anyone ever heard the word *Amish*? Does anyone know what it means?

- What does *fancy* mean? What is the opposite of *fancy*?

After You Read,

- Ask children what they think it would be like to live like the Amish. How would it differ from the way they live now?

- Let children pretend to be little Ruth and retell the story.

- **Invite children to make their own pretty peacock!**

Pretty Peacock

MATERIALS

- white paper coffee filter cones (1 and ¼ per child)
- colored markers or watercolor paints
- spray water bottle
- scissors
- copies of page 60 (1 per child)
- glue sticks
- pencils   **Note:** This activity will take two sessions to complete.

Session One:

1. Help children place the coffee filters on waxed paper or any material that will not soak up water.

2. With bright watercolor paints or markers, have children draw lines across the filters in a variety of colors so no white shows. With watercolors, use water sparingly so that colors remain intense. With colored markers, spray the coffee filters with water so that the entire surface is wet and the colors bleed together. Let dry overnight.

Session Two:

1. Have children fold their ¼ filter in half, to make a "pizza slice" shape. Have them fold it in half again, taking care to make the point at the top as neat as possible.

2. With scissors, show children how to cut the nonpointed side toward the middle and twist each resulting "leg" several times. Help children fold the pointy tip down to form a beak.

3. Fold the full coffee filter in half to form the back feathers. Glue the body onto the feathers and attach the peacock to the master sheet. Invite children to name their peacock at the bottom of the page!

Activities Across the Curriculum

Reading and Language Arts

✳ Discuss specific words and phrases that are used in this story: *working bee, frolic, womenfolk, shunned, elders, botherment, pleasured, white organdy cap.*

✳ Patricia Polacco shows the reader how the egg arrived in the pasture. Challenge children to find the answer in the illustrations.

Math and Science

✳ Shoofly Pie is a typical Amish dish. Make and eat Shoofly pie! (pie.allrecipes.com/AZ/ShflyPiV.asp)

✳ The Amish travel from place to place with a horse and buggy. How might a horse and buggy work? Invite children to use blocks, play wheels, and string to experiment with pulling different objects.

✳ Peacocks are very distinctive birds because of their tails. Discuss some other birds that have distinctive characteristics: pelican, mouth; ostrich, eggs; penguin, flightlessness.

✳ Visit Patricia Polacco's Web site: http://www.patriciapolacco.com

Art, Music, and Movement

✳ Create papier-mâché eggs the size of peacock eggs.

✳ Using fanciful, colored feathers found in a craft store, and an assortment of recycled objects, encourage children to create their own distinctive birds!

✳ Play music and have children move around like peacocks!

Book Links

■ *Hen Lake* by Mary Jane Auch (Holiday House, 1995). A delightful, tongue-in-cheek version of *Swan Lake.*

■ *Amish Christmas* by Richard Ammon (Atheneum, 1996). This beautifully illustrated book depicts the holiday customs in an Amish community.

■ *The Spooky Tail of Prewitt Peacock* by Bill Peet (Houghton Mifflin, 1973). Because of his strange-looking tail, other peacocks want Prewitt to leave—but they soon discover that the tail has its benefits!

■ *Selina and the Bear Paw Quilt* by Barbara Claasen Smucker (Dragonfly Press, 1999). Selina's father returns from the Civil War and decides that the family must leave for Canada to escape religious persecution, so grandmother carefully stitches them a quilt full of memories.

■ *Feathers and Fools* by Mem Fox (Harcourt, 1996). When two groups of birds become suspicious of one another, they prepare for a war—until they realize that peace will be lost forever.

Name _____

Just Plain Fancy

by Patricia Polacco

My fancy peacock's name is _____

20 Irresistible Reading-Response Projects Based on Favorite Picture Books   Scholastic Professional Books

Henry and Mudge in the Sparkle Days

by Cynthia Rylant • *Illustrated by Suçie Stevenson*

(Aladdin, 1997)

Henry and his dog, Mudge, enjoy a wintery holiday.

Before You Read, Ask Children:

- What do you think "sparkle days" might be?

- Does anyone here have a pet? What kind of pet?

- Do you like to play in snow?

- What do you need to wear to play outside in the snow?

After You Read,

- Point out that Henry and Mudge are great friends. Let children tell the qualities they appreciate in each other.

- Ask, *What sort of adventures do you think Henry and Mudge might have in the spring, summer, or autumn?*

- **Invite children to re-create Henry and Mudge's wintery scene!**

Mudge in the Snow

MATERIALS

- copies of page 63 (1 per child)
- crayons
- scissors
- scrap paper
- brass fasteners (1 per child)
- green paper in several shades
- glue
- puff paint (available in craft stores), sparkle glue, or glitter
- cotton balls
- pencils

1. Have children color Mudge and cut out a tail from scrap paper. Next, have them push a brass fastener through the tail and attach it to the paper so that Mudge can wag his tail.

2. Help children cut out several pine tree shapes from green paper to use as the background and glue them to the page.

3. With puff paint, sparkle glue, or glitter, children can create snow, stars, or snowflakes on their page.

4. Using pulled-apart cotton balls, help children glue blankets of snow to the ground or trees.

5. Children complete the sentence at the bottom of the page.

Activities Across the Curriculum

Reading and Language Arts

✳ Make a list on chart paper of "snow" words, such as *shimmer, glisten, sparkle, crunch,* and *cold*.

✳ In the last chapter, each member of the family wishes for something. Ask: *How do you make a wish? If you had a special wish, what would it be? If you were Mudge, what would you wish for?* List responses on chart paper.

Math and Science

✳ List and graph the pets children have.

✳ Have children consider why can you make snowballs with some kinds of snow and not others.

Art, Music, and Movement

✳ Have children cut out pictures from magazines and newspapers to create a collage of things you might find at a festival dinner.

✳ Make cut-and-fold snowflakes.

✳ Play music and invite children to pretend to be snowflakes falling from the sky!

Book Links

■ *Henry and Mudge in the Green Time* by Cynthia Rylant (Simon & Schuster, 1998). A summer adventure for Henry and Mudge includes a picnic, playing with the garden hose, and climbing to the top of a green hill.

■ *Henry and Mudge and the Best Day of All* by Cynthia Rylant (Simon & Schuster, 1995). Henry and Mudge celebrate Henry's birthday with a cake, a piñata and a fish tank.

■ *Henry and Mudge and the Long Weekend* by Cynthia Rylant (Simon & Schuster, 1998). Henry and Mudge turn a potentially boring weekend into an adventure by building a castle in the basement.

20 Irresistible Reading-Response Projects Based on Favorite Picture Books   Scholastic Professional Books

Name

Henry and Mudge in the Sparkle Days

by Cynthia Rylant

In the winter, I like to

Rechenka's Eggs

by Patricia Polacco

(Putnam, 1988)

Old Babushka is preparing eggs for the Easter Festival when she meets a very special goose.

Before You Read, Ask Children:

- How do you think the eggs on the cover of the book were made?

- Where is the Ukraine? Find it on a map or globe.

- What is a babushka? (grandmother)

After You Read,

- Ask, *How do you think Rechenka felt when the eggs fell and broke?*

- Ask, *What would you have named the new baby goose if you were Babushka?*

- **Invite children to create their own Pysanky egg!**

Goose's Pysanky

MATERIALS
- copies of pages 66–67 (one of each per child)
- crayons or markers
- scissors
- glue sticks
- pencils

1. Have children color their gosling page and then decorate the outside shell of their egg on the other page.

2. Help children cut out the two egg halves, fold along the dotted lines, and glue them to the edges of the egg shape on the gosling page (so that they open in the middle to reveal the gosling).

3. Invite children to complete the sentence at the bottom of the page.

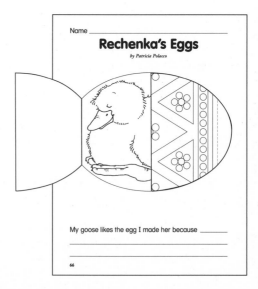

Name _____

Rechenka's Eggs
by Patricia Polacco

My goose likes the egg I made her because _____

_____

66

Activities Across the Curriculum

Reading and Language Arts

✳ List and define the Russian words found in the story: *Moskva* (Moscow), *kulich* (Easter bread), *pashka* (a spread of cheese, butter, and raisins), *niet* (no).

✳ Invite children to continue the story to tell what might happen next.

Math and Science

✳ Share nonfiction books about geese and migration, and make a list of goose facts.

✳ The buildings in this story have unique roofs with a vegetable nickname. Challenge children to guess what that nickname is. (*onion*)

✳ Find and make recipes for *kulich* and *pashka*. If there are Russian children in your class or school, involve them and their families in preparing these dishes with the class.

Art, Music, and Movement

✳ Have children cut an egg shape from white paper and use crayons to draw designs on the eggs. (Children should color all areas that they do not want to be black.) Add a generous amount of water to black tempera paint and have children paint their egg. Let dry.

✳ Have children cut a large egg shape out of black, blue, or purple paper. They can use white glue directly from the bottle to draw patterns and designs on the paper egg. Allow the glue to dry. Using oil pastels, children then color in the different sections of the egg design.

✳ Watch the Reading Rainbow video *Rechenka's Egg* and observe the author as she demonstrates how Pysanky is done. Then have children use crayons to make a wax design on hard-boiled eggs and dip the eggs into food coloring mixed with vinegar.

✳ Invite children to pretend to be goslings hatching from eggs!

Book Links

■ *Petunia* by Roger Duvoisin (Knopf, 2000). A goose wants to become wise, so she carries a book around with her!

■ *Goose* by Molly Bang (Scholastic, 1996). An egg accidentally rolls into the home of a woodchuck family.

■ *Flight of the Snow Geese* by Deborah King (Orchard, 1998). A lyrical description of the flight of the snow geese from the tundra to warmer climates.

■ *The Bird's Gift* by Eric Kimmel (Holiday House, 1999). When villagers save a flock of birds from freezing, they are rewarded with a gift of finely decorated eggs.

Name _____

Rechenka's Eggs
by Patricia Polacco

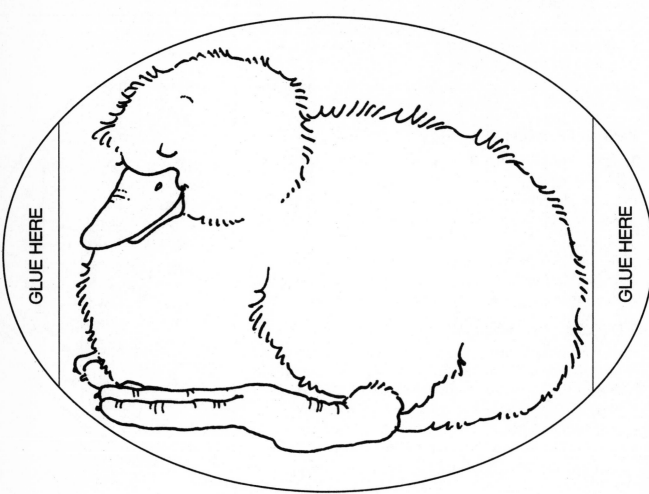

My goose likes the egg I made her because

_____

_____

20 Irresistible Reading-Response Projects Based on Favorite Picture Books   Scholastic Professional Books

Rechenka's Eggs

CUT IN HALF ALONG THIS LINE

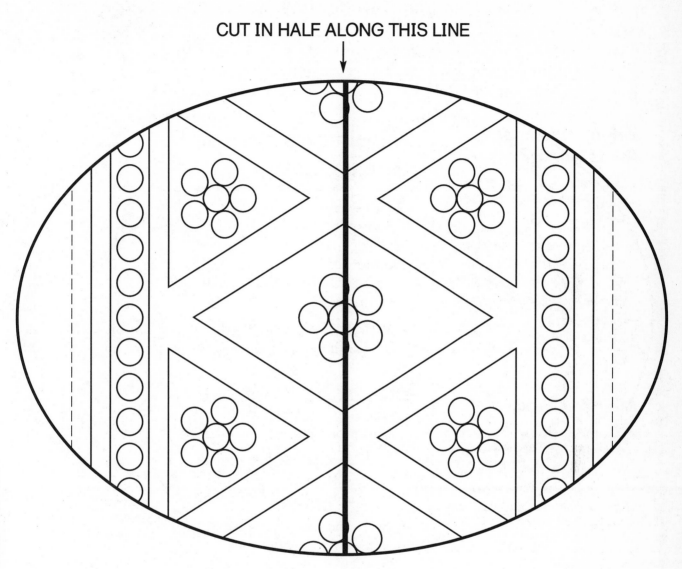

Poppleton

by Cynthia Rylant • Illustrated by Mark Teague

(Scholastic, 1997)

Poppleton the pig and his friends share adventures in this simple chapter book.

Before You Read, Ask Children:

- By looking at the cover of the book, what can you tell me about Poppleton?

- There are three chapters in this book: "Neighbors," "The Library," and "The Pill." From those titles, what do you think might happen in each story?

- What is a neighbor? What is a library?

After You Read,

- Discuss the chapter about neighbors. Ask, *Why did Poppleton squirt Cherry Sue with the hose? What would you have done in that situation if you were Poppleton?*

- Invite children to name adjectives that describe Poppleton.

- **Invite children to create a Poppleton portrait!**

Poppleton's Portrait

MATERIALS

- page 71 copied onto pink construction paper (1 per child)
- copies of page 70 (1 per child)
- scissors
- glue
- black buttons or dry black beans
- cut-apart pink egg cartons (1 cup per child)
- scrap paper

1. Have children cut out Poppleton's face, fold his ears forward, and glue it to their blank page, being careful not to glue the ears.

2. Children can then glue on black button or bean eyes and the egg-carton nose.

3. Invite children use scrap paper to dress Poppleton in a tie or hat to add color and personality!

4. Have children complete the sentence at the bottom of the page.

egg carton cup

Activities Across the Curriculum

Reading and Language Arts

✳ Make a list on chart paper of words that describe or are associated with pigs: *snout*, *sloppy*, *pink*, *mud*, and so on.

✳ Have children think of other pigs they are familiar with, such as Wilbur, Babe, and the Three Little Pigs.

✳ Introduce and discuss pig-related idioms, such as *go hog-wild*, *pick of the litter*, or *make a pig of yourself*.

✳ Poppleton went to the library to read. Talk together about other things you can find at the library besides books (magazines, newspapers, books on tape, videos).

Math and Science

✳ As a class, share nonfiction books about pigs and, together, create a list of pig facts.

✳ Ask children, *In the chapter "The Pill," how many cakes did Poppleton and Fillmore eat?*

Art, Music, and Movement

✳ Make "mud paintings" with finger paint!

✳ Play This Little Piggy.

✳ Invite children to imitate how a pig might walk!

Book Links

■ *Poppleton Forever* by Cynthia Rylant (Blue Sky Press, 1998). Poppleton catches a cold, plants a tree, and attempts to hang wallpaper.

■ *Poppleton Everyday* by Cynthia Rylant (Blue Sky Press, 1998). Poppleton continues his adventures by going sailing, trying out beds before he buys one, and stargazing with a friend.

■ *Poppleton in Spring* by Cynthia Rylant (Blue Sky Press, 1999). Poppleton tries out a new tent, attempts to buy a bicycle, and does some spring cleaning.

Name _____

Poppleton
by Cynthia Rylant

I might like Poppleton for a pet because

_____

_____

20 Irresistible Reading-Response Projects Based on Favorite Picture Books   Scholastic Professional Books

Poppleton

Harry the Dirty Dog

by Gene Zion • *Illustrated by Margaret Bloy Graham*

(HarperCollins, 1976)

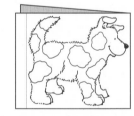

Harry hates to have a bath, so he runs away—and gets so dirty that even his family can't recognize him!

Before You Read, Ask Children:

- Do you like to take baths?
- How do dogs get dirty? What other things do they do that get them into trouble?
- How do you give a dog a bath?

After You Read,

- Make a list on chart paper of all the things Harry saw on his adventure.
- Write a collaborative letter to Gene Zion. You might begin with "We like Harry because..."
- **Invite children to create "before and after" Harry portraits!**

Harry: Before and After

MATERIALS
- copy of pages 74–75 (1 of each per child)
- crayons
- scissors
- glue sticks
- pencils

1. Have children color Harry on one side as a dark dog with white spots, and on the other as a white dog with dark spots.

2. Children cut around the solid lines of the dog sheet and fold the sheet in the middle (between the two dogs).

3. Children glue the two edges together and fold along the line. Glue in place to the master sheet. (See diagram.)

4. Children complete the sentences at the bottom of the page.

5. Children can then flip Harry back and forth as they retell the story.

---

74 Name _____

Harry the Dirty Dog *by Gene Zion*

People might like baths because _____

People might not like baths because _____

Activities Across the Curriculum

Reading and Language Arts

* Have children dictate instructions on how to get clean or how to wash a dog. Record their ideas on chart paper.

* Harry was happy to be home with his family again. Brainstorm a list on chart paper of things that make the class happy.

Math and Science

* Show children a box of dog bones and have them guess how many bones are in the box. Record the guesses and then count the bones!

* When Harry was traveling through the city, he saw many things—some of which are no longer used. Let children try to guess what they are and what replaced them.

Art, Music, and Movement

* Have children use waxed paper and brown finger paint to "play in the mud" and get dirty! They can trace Harry in the paint or pudding.

* Sing a variation of "BINGO":

    There was a little dirty dog
    And Harry was his name-O,
    H-A-R-R-Y,
    H-A-R-R-Y,
    H-A-R-R-Y,
    And Harry was his name-O.

Book Links

- *Harry and the Lady Next Door* by Gene Zion (HarperCollins, 1978). Harry does everything he can to get the lady next door to stop singing!

- *Harry by the Sea* by Gene Zion (HarperCollins, 1987). Harry gets covered in seaweed—and is mistaken for a sea serpent.

- *No Roses for Harry* by Gene Zion (HarperCollins, 1976). Grandmother's birthday present to Harry is a sweater covered in roses!

Name _____

Harry the Dirty Dog *by Gene Zion*

GLUE HERE

People might like baths because _____

People might not like baths because _____

20 Irresistible Reading-Response Projects Based on Favorite Picture Books   Scholastic Professional Books

Harry the Dirty Dog

GLUE THIS FLAP DOWN

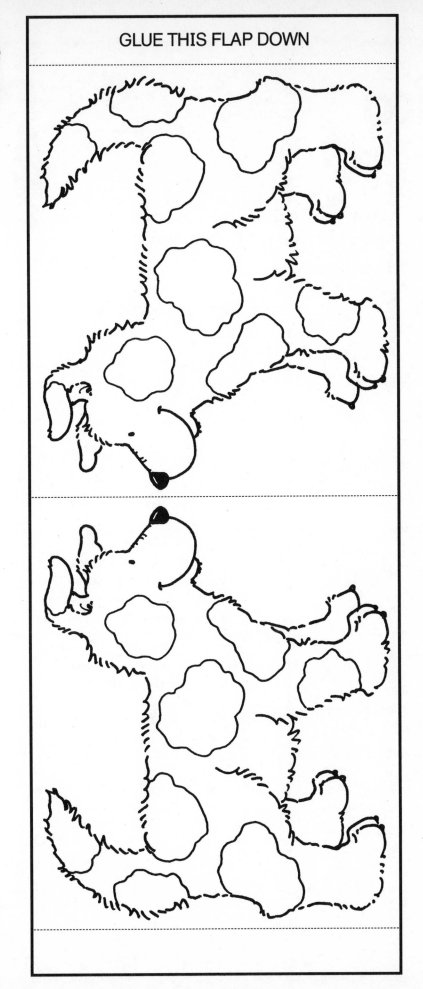

GLUE THIS FLAP DOWN

Yoko

by Rosemary Wells

(Hyperion, 2001)

When Yoko's classmates make fun of her lunch, her teacher encourages the class to bring in their family's favorite foods.

Before You Read, Ask Children:

- What is sushi?

- Where can you get sushi? Have you ever eaten it? How do you think it is made?

- What is your favorite food?

- What would you like to taste but have never had a chance to try?

After You Read,

- Have volunteers role-play the teacher and Yoko. Ask, *If you were the teacher, what would you have said or done to make Yoko feel better?*

- List the foods mentioned in the story and help children decide what country each food comes from. Children can take turns locating those places on a map.

- **Invite children to make a sushi lunch!**

Sushi for Lunch

MATERIALS

- copies of page 78 (1 per child)
- 4- by 5-inch pieces of light-colored construction paper or subtly shaded wallpaper (1 per child)
- glue
- pencils
- crayons
- magazines
- scissors
- 2-inch dark green paper circles (2 per child)
- colorful paper scraps
- dry rice
- 1- by 2-inch pieces of craft foam (2 per child, available in craft stores)
- raffia or yarn
- pencils

1. Have children glue their construction paper or wallpaper to the left side of the place mat. On the other side of the place mat, have children write, draw, or cut out and glue pictures from magazines of their favorite lunches.

2. To make rice rolls, have children put glue on each green circle and cut and add small triangular "vegetables" (from scrap paper) to the center of the glued surfaces, and sprinkle dry rice on the rest of the circle.

3. To make sushi, children use their craft foam and a piece of wallpaper cut to the same dimensions as the foam. Have them add a small amount of glue to hold the paper and foam together. Show children how to wrap raffia or yarn around each piece of sushi. Glue the sushi and rolls on the left side of the place mat. (See cover of this book.)

4. Children complete the sentence at the bottom of the page.

Activities Across the Curriculum

Reading and Language Arts

✳ Encourage children to bring from home a favorite recipe and create a class cookbook of family foods, or have children create menus of foods commonly enjoyed in their home.

✳ Share a favorite recipe that uses rice and write it on chart paper.

Math and Science

✳ Sushi rice is different from other types of rice. Compare different types of rice and discuss similarities and differences in size, shape, color, and use.

✳ Compare the amount of water, the temperature, and any specific cooking instructions needed to prepare different types of rice. Why do children think these vary?

✳ If a child uses chopsticks at home, have him or her show the class how to use them. Children might take turns practicing by picking up various classroom objects. Discuss which items were the easiest or hardest to pick up and why.

Art, Music, and Movement

✳ Using rice in different textures and colors, help children make mosaic pictures. Spread a thin layer of glue on a sheet of sturdy paper and add rice as desired.

✳ Ask volunteers to make up a "Friendly Song" of their own and teach it to the class.

✳ Provide an assortment of cans, bottles, plastic containers, and tubes. Have children put a spoonful of rice into each before sealing them and turning them into instruments! Take turns listening to the different sounds produced and making up different rhythms.

Book Links

■ *Cleversticks* by Bernald Ashley (Random House, 1995). Ling Sung is concerned about going to school, but his ability to use chopsticks gives him a new appreciation for teaching and learning.

■ *How My Parents Learned to Eat* by Ina R. Friedman (Houghton Mifflin, 1984). When a young American sailor dates a Japanese girl, each secretly learns how to use chopsticks and silverware.

■ *Watch Out for the Chicken Feet In Your Soup* by Tomie de Paola (Econoclad, 1999). A young boy is embarrassed by his grandmother and her old-country style of cooking.

■ *Mama Provi and the Pot of Rice* by Sylvia Rosa-Casanova (Atheneum, 1997). When Mama Provi takes chicken with rice to her sick granddaughter, each neighbor adds his or her own cultural touch to her visit.

Name _____

Yoko
by Rosemary

If Yoko had lunch with me, I would share my _____

20 Irresistible Reading-Response Projects Based on Favorite Picture Books Scholastic Professional Books